DK findout!
eyewonder
Dinosaurs

 Penguin Random House

Managing editor Laura Gilbert
Managing art editor Diane Peyton Jones
Producer, Pre-production Gillian Reid
Senior producer Charlotte Oliver
Special Sales creative project manager
Michelle Baxter

DK INDIA
Project editor Suneha Dutta
Art editor Shreya Sadhan
Senior editor Shatarupa Chaudhuri
Senior art editor Nishesh Batnagar
Managing editor Alka Thakur Hazarika
Managing art editor Romi Chakraborty
DTP designer Bimlesh Tiwary

First published in Great Britain in 2001
This edition published in Great Britain in 2015
by Dorling Kindersley Limited
80 Strand, London WC2R 0RL

Material in this publication was
previously published in:
Eyewonder Dinosaurs (2013)
Copyright © 2001, © 2013, © 2015
Dorling Kindersley Limited
A Penguin Random House Company

001–290050–June/2015

All rights reserved. No part of this publication
may be reproduced, stored in or introduced into a retrieval
system, or transmitted, in any form, or by any means,
(electronic, mechanical, photocopying, recording,
or otherwise), without the prior written permission
of the copyright owners.

A CIP catalogue record for this book is available
from the British Library

ISBN 978-0-2412-4389-3

Printed and bound in Italy by L.E.G.O. S.p.A.

A WORLD OF IDEAS:
SEE ALL THERE IS TO KNOW

Contents

2-3 What is a dinosaur?
4-5 Dinosaur times
6-7 Skeletons
8-9 Fossils
10-11 Dinosaur footprints
12-13 Different dinosaurs
14-15 Dinosaur world
16-17 Little and large
18-19 On the move
20-21 Plant eaters
22-23 *Iguanodon*
24-25 Hungry herds
26-27 Meat eaters
28-29 *Allosaurus*
30-31 Hunters
32-33 Activities
34-35 Danger
36-37 Facts match
38-39 Which way?
40-41 True or false?
42-43 Tough tactics
44-45 *Kentrosaurus*
46-47 Camouflage
48-49 Courtship
50-51 Nests and nurseries
52-53 High flyers
54-55 *Eudimorphodon*
56-57 Under the waves
58-59 *Albertonectes*
60-61 Brain power
62-63 Dinosaur details
64-65 Death of the dinosaurs
66-67 Digging up dinosaurs
68-69 Building dinosaurs
70-71 Index
72 Acknowledgements

1

What is a dinosaur?

Dinosaurs roamed the Earth for hundreds of millions of years, then mysteriously died out. They were reptiles that varied from fierce killers to gentle plant eaters. A group of dinosaurs evolved into birds – they are the living dinosaurs.

Lizard legs
Like modern reptiles, most dinosaurs had scaly skin, a long tail, teeth, and claws. Today's reptiles have legs that splay sideways. Dinosaurs had straight legs directly below their bodies.

Sharp teeth lined the powerful jaws of many meat-eating dinosaurs.

Short arms were used for grasping prey.

Feathered friends
Scientists believe that all modern birds are descended from dinosaurs, such as *Velociraptor* and *Archaeopteryx*. Scientists study birds to try to guess how dinosaurs behaved.

Birds have feet like those of many dinosaurs.

Motherly love
Clues to how dinosaurs behaved also come from today's reptiles. Crocodiles are survivors from prehistoric times. They feed their babies and protect them. Some dinosaurs probably did this, too.

Creature features

Dinosaurs had different features to equip them for survival. Meat-eating dinosaurs had sharp teeth and claws for hunting. Some plant eaters grew to vast sizes. Others had natural weapons such as horns.

Some dinosaurs had a row of spines along their back, from head to tail.

Large tail helped dinosaurs to balance as they leant forwards.

Most dinosaurs had bumpy, scaly skin.

Muscular hind legs allowed meat eaters to chase their prey.

Dinosaur facts

- Dinosaurs were the biggest land animals of all time, although some whales, such as the blue whale, are larger.

- Flying reptiles lived at the same time as the dinosaurs.

- There were prehistoric swimming reptiles that lived alongside dinosaurs.

Dinosaur times

The age of the dinosaurs is known as the Mesozoic era. This stretched from 248 to 65 million years ago. It divides into three separate time spans: the Triassic, the Jurassic, and the Cretaceous.

The Triassic period lasted from 252 to 201 million years ago.

Triassic world
At the start of the Mesozoic era, the continents were joined together into one supercontinent – Pangaea. This was surrounded by a massive ocean called Panthalassa.

Small beginnings
The Triassic world saw the first small dinosaurs. Like most early dinosaurs, meat-eating *Herrerasaurus* (he-rair-a-sore-us) walked on its hind legs.

Jurassic world
Over millions of years, Pangaea split into two continents, Gondwana and Laurasia. As these drifted apart, different groups of dinosaurs evolved on each continent.

The Jurassic period lasted from 201 to 145 million years ago.

The Cretaceous period lasted from 145 to 66 million years ago.

Cretaceous world
The continents continued to drift apart and the Earth began to look like it does today. The vast mountain ranges of the Andes and the Rockies were formed.

Land of the giants
Late in the Jurassic period, giant sauropods roamed in conifer forests, and *Stegosaurus* (steg-oh-sore-us) ate low-growing plants. Ichthyosaurs (ick-thee-oh-sores) and other reptiles swam in the seas.

Dinosaur heyday
The great variety of Cretaceous dinosaurs included horned plant eaters like *Styracosaurus* (sty-rack-oh-saw-russ) and huge meat eaters such as *Tyrannosaurus rex* (tie-ran-oh-sore-us recks).

Skeletons

A skeleton tells a story. Teeth or bony beaks give information about what dinosaurs probably ate. Features such as horns show how they defended themselves. Small braincases tell us which dinosaurs had small brains!

Narrow jaw with sharp teeth

Small sprinter
A fossilized skeleton shows that *Coelophysis* (see-low-fye-sis) had long legs for its small size. It was 3 m (9 ft) long and could run fast.

Spiky plant eater
A Late Jurassic dinosaur, *Stegosaurus* (steg-oh-sore-us) was probably about 3 m (9 ft) high. It had bony plates along its back. Its spiky tail was flexible and most likely used for defence.

Bony plate

Small head

Long hind legs

Short front legs

Tail spike

Tyrannosaurus rex could have swallowed a person whole.

Stiff, heavy tail helped balance.

Powerful hind legs

Large head with huge, hinged jaws

Massive meat eater
Meat eaters such as *Tyrannosaurus rex* (tie-ran-oh-sore-us recks) had massive jaws. They could swallow large mouthfuls of meat.

Bird-like dinosaur
A fossilized skeleton of *Struthiomimus* (strooth-ee-oh-meem-us) shows that it had features in common with today's ostrich. These include a small head with a narrow beak, a long neck, and powerful hind limbs.

Jurassic giant
The longest of all the dinosaurs, sauropods such as *Diplodocus* (di-plod-o-kus) had small skulls containing small brains! Despite its length, *Diplodocus* weighed no more than two large elephants.

From head to tail, vast *Diplodocus* measured about 27.2 m (90 ft).

Horned head
The Late Cretaceous *Triceratops* (try-serra-tops) was hunted by *Tyrannosaurus rex*. It probably used its horns to defend itself. A plant eater, it had a tough, toothless beak.

Fossils

In rare cases the soft parts of an animal's body, such as its skin, may form fossils.

Edmontosaurus skin

This fossil shows the skin of a dinosaur called *Edmontosaurus*. It formed when the dinosaur's skin was pressed into soft mud.

8   **Why not find out more?**

Ichthyosaur skull

The ichthyosaurs were the largest sea-dwelling reptiles. The fossil shows that the animal had large eyes and long jaws lined with teeth. They looked just like dolphins, but studies of *Ichthyosaurus* ear bones show that it didn't have the highly sensitive hearing that dolphins have and couldn't detect objects in the water by using echoes (echolocation).

Footprints of dinosaurs

10 **Why not find out more?**

Dinosaur footprints

Sometimes, the footprints, eggs, dung, and nests, of ancient creatures turn into fossils. These are known as trace fossils, because they are traces or imprints (signs) of an animal's life rather than its fossilized body parts. Fossilized dinosaur tracks, such as these in Arizona, USA, help scientists to work out how fast these extinct reptiles walked and ran.

Different dinosaurs

Dinosaurs are divided into two main groups, according to their hip bones. Some had hips arranged like a lizard's and others had hips arranged like a bird's.

Lizard like
This group includes two-legged meat eaters such as *Tyrannosaurus rex* (tie-ran-oh-sore-us recks) as well as plant-eating sauropods like *Diplodocus* (di-plod-o-kus).

Giant Saltasaurus (sal-tah-sore-us) lived in the Late Cretaceous period.

Bird bones
All bird-hipped dinosaurs were plant eaters. Some of the most familiar faces of the dinosaur world are found in this group!

Iguanodon (ig-wahn-oh-don) lived in the Cretaceous period. It grew to 9.3 m (30 ft) long.

Dinosaur facts

- Strangely, experts think that today's birds evolved from lizard-hipped dinosaurs, not bird-hipped dinosaurs!

- To date, over 1,000 species of dinosaur have been found and named. Every few months more are discovered.

Tyrannosaurus rex (tie-ran-oh-sore-us recks) lived in the Late Cretaceous period. It stood over 6 m (20 ft) tall.

Gallimimus (gally-meem-us) lived in the Late Cretaceous period. It probably reached speeds of 70 kph (43 mph).

Triceratops (try-serra-tops) lived in the Cretaceous period. Its three sharp horns grew up to 90 cm (3 ft) long.

Stegosaurus (steg-oh-sore-us) lived in the Late Jurassic period. It had a toothless beak and a tiny brain!

Feeding on ferns
No grass grew in the prehistoric landscape. Instead, many types of fern thrived on the forest floor. *Stegosaurus* (steg-oh-sore-us) munched on ferns and seed cones.

Dinosaur facts
● Duck-billed dinosaurs could chew through really tough plants because their jaws and teeth were so powerful.

● Flowering plants spread more quickly than other plants, and soon became widespread throughout the world.

Dinosaur world

The dinosaurs' world was generally hot and sunny. There were areas of desert, and forests of conifers and ferns. Later, the first flowering plants appeared.

Insect survivor
Some familiar insects fluttered in prehistoric skies. Modern dragonflies look very much like this fossilized dragonfly, which lived 140 million years ago.

Cycads
While dinosaurs ruled the world, palm-like plants called cycads were plentiful. They still grow in some parts of the world today, although they are rare.

Flower feast
Flowering plants, such as magnolias, first appeared in the Cretaceous period. They were probably eaten by plant-eating dinosaurs.

Prehistoric puzzle
Monkey-puzzle trees thrived on the Earth long before the dinosaurs. Today's monkey puzzles are related to these.

Mammal
One of the first small mammals, *Megazostrodon* (mega-zos-troh-don) lived alongside early dinosaurs. This furry model is based on a tiny skeleton.

Low life
Small meat eaters such as *Compsognathus* (komp-sog-nay-thus) hunted lizards and insects. They ran fast, chasing their prey through low-growing plants.

Mighty meat eater
Tyrannosaurus rex (tie-ran-oh-sore-us recks) was one of the largest meat-eating dinosaurs. It would have been tall enough to peer into an upstairs window.

Small but speedy
Compsognathus (komp-sog-nay-thus) was the size of a turkey. It may have been small, but its long legs meant it was built for speed. It could sprint fast after prey.

Little and large

Dinosaurs of many shapes and sizes roamed the prehistoric Earth. They varied from small, bird-like dinosaurs to the most enormous creatures ever to live on land. Largest of all were the giant, long-necked sauropods.

Sky-scraping sauropods
Huge sauropods such as *Barosaurus* (barrow-sore-us) could nibble leaves from treetops as tall as a five-storey building. It relied on its size and strength to defend itself against predators.

On the move

Among the dinosaurs, the fastest were probably two-legged ornithomimids – the "ostrich mimics". The four-legged, heavy-footed types, unlike what scientists thought earlier, could also move quickly. There were athletic dinosaurs as well.

Plodding along
Although they had huge bodies and short legs, sauropods like *Saltasaurus* (sal-tah-sore-us) could move quickly, probably faster than humans.

Gallimimus might have run at 70 kph

Taking the fast track
Gallimimus, meaning "chicken mimic", may have been the speediest dinosaur. With its light body and long legs, it could sprint away from predators.

Fancy footwork
From footprints, it is possible to see if a dinosaur was two-legged or four-legged. They also show whether a dinosaur was walking, trotting, or running.

Road runners
Like ostriches, *Gallimimus* (gally-meem-us) had powerful legs for striding out. Unlike ostriches they had long tails, which helped them to keep their balance.

(43 mph), which is faster than a winning racehorse.

OOPS A DAISY!
Large, meat-eating dinosaurs could probably run fast. However, their short arms could not break a fall if they lost their balance. An *Allosaurus* (allo-sore-us) found with 14 cracked ribs, probably injured itself whilst running after prey.

Gentle giant
A huge sauropod, *Barosaurus* (barrow-sore-us) had a long, muscly neck for reaching food. It may have reared up on its thick hind legs to reach foliage high up in the treetops. A long tail helped it to keep its balance.

Plant eaters

Sauropods were the biggest plant eaters ever to walk the Earth. Most lived during the Jurassic period. Smaller plant-eating dinosaurs flourished before and after these giants existed.

Peg-like teeth

Tearing teeth
For stripping leafy twigs, *Diplodocus* (di-plod-o-kus) had teeth right at the front of its jaws. Perhaps this sauropod ate conifers, cycads, ferns, and tree-ferns.

Beak billed
Hadrosaurs (had-row-sores) had duck-like beaks for ripping up vegetation. They had more than 40 rows of teeth. They probably ate pine needles, seeds, twigs, and low, leafy plants.

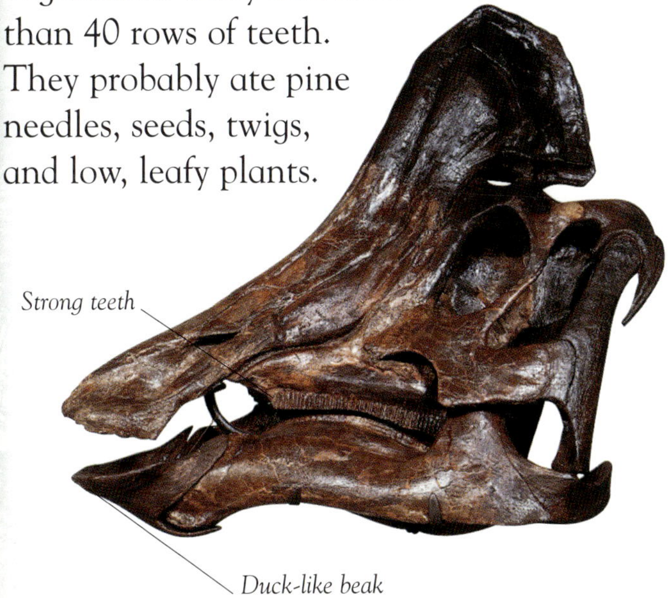

Strong teeth

Duck-like beak

BOULDER EATERS?
Sauropods such as *Apatosaurus* (a-pat-oh-sore-us) ate huge amounts of greenery each day to support their massive size. They did not chew the tough plants before swallowing. Earlier, some scientists thought that they gulped down stones to grind up the food in their stomach!

Ground grazer
Whilst sauropods munched treetop greenery, other dinosaurs tackled low-growing plants. *Edmontonia* (ed-mon-toe-nee-a) ate mainly ferns and mosses.

The skull was tall and narrow, with high-set eyes that provided a wide field of vision.

Iguanodon's beak was made of hard keratin. This is the same material found in bird beaks and human fingernails.

Iguanodon

Iguanodon was an ornithopod dinosaur (bulky plant eater). It was as big as an elephant and spent most of its time walking on all four limbs, feeding on low-growing plants.

Iguanodon had a long, spike-shaped thumb. It may have used this to defend itself against predators.

22   Why not find out more?

The weight of the head and upper body was balanced by a long, stiff, and heavy tail.

Iguanodon, means "iguana teeth". It was given this name because its teeth looked like those of an iguana.

Most of Iguanodon's weight was supported by its massively built hind limbs.

www.dkfindout.com

Dinosaur facts

● Herd dinosaurs probably had excellent eyesight, hearing, and sense of smell to detect danger.

● Hadrosaurs are also known as duck-billed dinosaurs.

● Herds may have been noisy. Calls to each other probably warned of nearby predators.

Forest friends

Giant herds of hadrosaurs, such as *Corythosaurus* (ko-rith-oh-sore-us), roamed through Cretaceous forests, living mostly in places with firm and dry ground.

Duck-billed dinosaurs could store food in their cheeks, like hamsters.

Hungry herds

Some plant-eating dinosaurs formed herds. There was safety in numbers, and they could warn each other of predators. They may also have travelled together to find food.

Hiding in the crowd
Travelling as a herd makes it difficult for predators to pick out just one animal. Today, as many as one million wildebeest herd together.

Some hadrosaurs had head crests in weird and wonderful shapes.

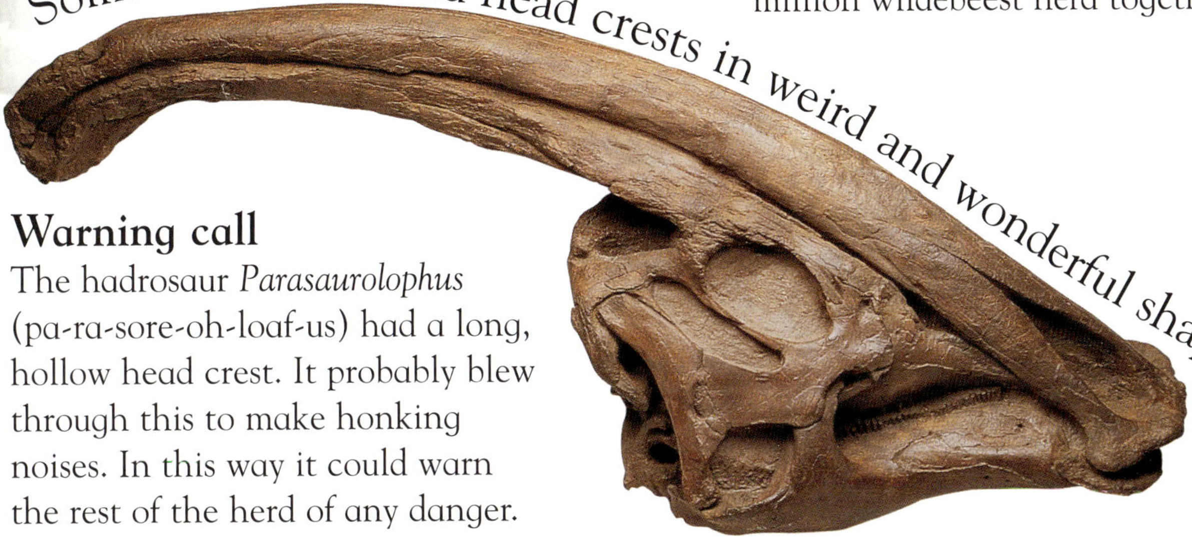

Warning call
The hadrosaur *Parasaurolophus* (pa-ra-sore-oh-loaf-us) had a long, hollow head crest. It probably blew through this to make honking noises. In this way it could warn the rest of the herd of any danger.

Horned defence
Herds could have used group defence tactics. *Triceratops* (try-serra-tops) may have formed a circle for protection, turning their horns outwards to face an attacker.

Following the tail in front
Some herds of plant-eating dinosaurs may have trudged vast distances to find good grazing land. Herds of *Pachyrhinosaurus* (pack-ee-rye-no-sore-us) may have walked from Canada to northern Alaska each spring to feed on large-leafed plants.

Styracosaurus had sharp spikes on its head for defence.

Meat eaters

During the Cretaceous period, gigantic, meat-eating dinosaurs ruled the land. Other creatures had to be on their guard against these ferocious hunters!

Big and mighty
Tyrannosaurus rex (tie-ran-oh-sore-us recks) was one of the biggest meat eaters to live on the Earth.

Dinosaur facts

- *Spinosaurus* (spine-oh-saw-russ) was one of the biggest predators. It ate fish, flying reptiles, and small dinosaurs.

- The flesh-eating dinosaur *Giganotosaurus* (jig-anno-toe-sore-us) was huge, weighing an enormous eight tonnes!

Fearsome fish-eater

Suchomimus (sue-koh-mime-us) was a vast, fish-eating dinosaur with a head like a crocodile! It probably waded out into rivers and lakes to catch fish with its jaws or clawed hands.

Long, powerful jaws were lined with more than 100 razor-sharp teeth.

Crocodile smile

Like *Suchomimus*, *Baryonyx* (barry-on-icks) lived near water and ate fish. In addition to snappy jaws, *Baryonyx* had a large, curved claw for spearing fish.

Scary skull

A relative of *Tyrannosaurus rex*, *Albertosaurus* (al-bur-toe-sore-us) was a frightening sight! It had enormous curved teeth, and could move quickly after its prey.

INTO THE JAWS

Tyrannosaurus rex was a fierce hunter. It had up to 60 teeth that were as sharp and long as knives, and its jaws were strong enough to crush bones. Although it was very heavy, it could probably sprint over long distances, and use its short arms to grip its victims while it ate them!

Allosaurus

Allosaurus belonged to a group of meat eaters called theropods. With its knifelike teeth and strong, sharp claws, *Allosaurus* was one of the most common of the big predators of the Late Jurassic age. It specialized in attacking and eating super-sized animals, such as the rhino-sized *Stegosaurus*. Like many theropods, *Allosaurus* was probably a scavenger as well as a hunter, feeding on any dead animal it could find as well as eating dinosaurs that it killed.

Bony projections above the eye sockets of Allosaurus's skull probably supported a pair of short horns.

Allosaurus's powerful jaws were lined with more than 70 sharp-edged teeth.

Allosaurus used hooked claws on its three-fingered arms to grapple with struggling prey, pinning down victims to stop them escaping.

Tooth marks on *Allosaurus* bones reveal that these dinosaurs sometimes ate each other.

Why not find out more?

Although Allosaurus was a large dinosaur, it was much more lightly built than the most well-known theropod, Tyrannosaurus.

Allosaurus held its long, heavy tail outstretched to help balance itself as it ran.

Like nearly all theropod dinosaurs, Allosaurus walked on its two hind legs.

Allosaurus ran on its three strong main toes. It also had a very small fourth toe on the inner side of each foot.

Sickle-shaped claw

Hunters

Some of the smaller, meat-eating dinosaurs snapped up prey such as lizards, small mammals, or eggs. Others probably hunted in groups to overpower larger victims. Hunting in this way demanded teamwork and intelligence.

Terrible talon
Velociraptor (vell-oss-ee-rap-tor) had a large, sharp claw on the second toe of each hind foot. Held off the ground for walking, the claw could sweep out like a flick knife to slash prey.

Pack attack!
A savage hunter, *Velociraptor* may have used group tactics to single out and attack victims. Raptors were well equipped to kill, with sharp claws, toothy jaws, and agile bodies. These intelligent dinosaurs may have ambushed their prey as lions do.

Defend or die!
All was not over for *Protoceratops* (pro-toe-serra-tops). Its sharp beak was a useful weapon, as it charged its enemy like a small rhinoceros.

Flexible neck for swooping down on prey

Present-day packs
Today's pack animals perhaps hunt in a similar way to those dinosaurs that hunted in groups. In a wolf pack, some members herd while others lie in wait to ambush prey.

Successful scavengers
Coelophysis (see-low-fye-siss) were nimble, meat-eating dinosaurs. They were not fussy eaters, and snapped up any creature they were able to swallow!

Dinosaur facts
- It is likely that *Velociraptor* used its muscular legs to stamp on small prey, like secretary birds do today.
- *Coelophysis* had hollow bones, and was a light, agile, and speedy predator.
- *Velociraptor* and *Protoceratops* both lived during the Cretaceous era.

Hundred *Hypsilophodon* fossils have been found in a single site in Britain.

Activities

34-35
Danger

36-37
Facts match

38-39
Which way?

40-41
True or false?

www.dkfindout.com 33

Facts match

How much do you know about the dinosaur world? Each of these dinosaurs can be found in the book – read the clues and see if you can identify the correct dinosaur.

My sharp beak is a useful weapon as I charge at my enemy like a rhinoceros. See page 30

I am one of the first small mammals. I lived alongside the early dinosaurs. See page 15

I have two pairs of flippers. I flap these like wings to glide through water. See page 57

Although I am the longest of all dinosaurs, I weigh no more than two large elephants. See page 7

I have three sharp horns that grow up to 90 cm (3 ft) long. See page 13

I am a bulky dinosaur, and about the length of a truck. See page 43

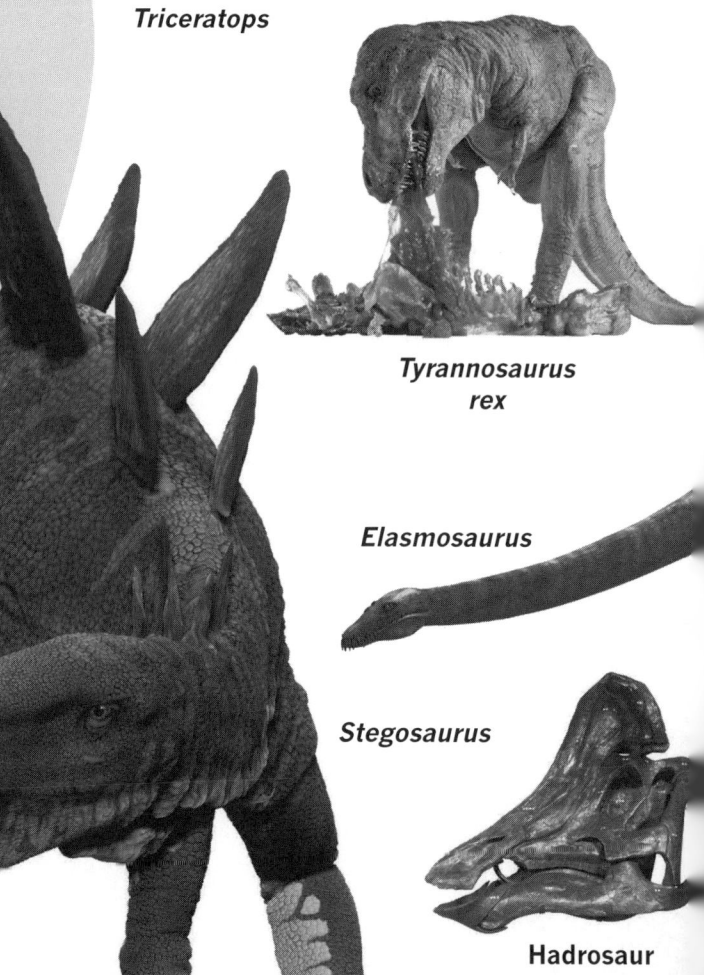

Protoceratops

Struthiomimus skeleton

Triceratops

Tyrannosaurus rex

Elasmosaurus

Stegosaurus

Hadrosaur

Megazostrodon

Barosaurus

Diplodocus skull

Stegosaurus skeleton

Coelophysis skeleton

Troodon

Styracosaurus skull

Gallimimus

Iguanodon

My name means "wounding tooth". I also have very large eyes. See page 61

I have bony plates along my back. My spiky tail is flexible. See page 6

I am one of the largest meat-eating dinosaurs. I am tall enough to peer into an upstairs window. See page 16

My legs are long for my small size. I am 3 m (9 ft) long and can run fast. See page 6

I use my spiky thumb to stab my enemy when attacked. See page 43

I have a duck-like beak and more than 40 rows of teeth. See page 21

A lifesize copy of my skeleton is displayed in a New York museum. See page 69

I have a vast neck frill that is fringed with six spikes. See page 49

I have features in common with today's ostrich, such as a small head with a narrow beak. See page 7

My name means "chicken mimic". I have a light body and long legs. See page 16

Which way?

Help the *Maisaura* find her eggs by answering the questions correctly and finding the path through the forest.

Tyrannosaurus rex

redwoods

conifers

Which of these reptiles lived in the seas?
See page 56

Oviraptor

In Jurassic forests, the trees were…
See page 5

Liopleurodon

warm and wet

oaks

covered in snow

The dinosaurs' world was mostly…
See page 15

START

Up to 600

Up to 60

straw

A *Tyrannosaurus rex* had how many teeth?
See page 27

16

turkey

Some dinosaurs made nests for their eggs with...
See page 51

sparrow

mud

trees

A *Compsognathus* was the size of a...
See page 16

pigeon

FINISH

True or false?

It's time to go back to the dinosaur age and see if you can spot what is true and what is false in this mini quiz.

Stegosaurus was very brainy.
See page 13

Male Pentaceratops used their frill to attract a mate.
See page 49

A duck-billed dinosaur could store food in its neck.
See page 24

Features such as horns show how dinosaurs defended themselves.
See page 6

Magnolias first appeared in the Cretaceous period.
See page 15

The *Heterodontosaurus* was a hunter, and used its sharp teeth to attack its rivals and prey.

Tough tactics

Plant-eating dinosaurs were particularly at risk from predators. They needed protection from hungry meat eaters like this huge *Giganotosaurus* (jig-anno-toe-sore-us). Some had heavy coats of armour. Others made weapons of their claws, tails, or horns.

Dinosaur facts

- Lots of the smaller dinosaurs did not have methods of defence. If attacked, they would simply run away!
- *Ankylosaurus* (an-kye-low-saw-rus) was covered in armour plating. Even its eyelids were protected! Only its underbelly was free from protection.

Large, sharp teeth easily pierced the tough skin of victims.

Sharp thumb
Iguanodon (ig-whan-oh-don) was a peaceful plant eater, but it could use its spiky thumb to stab its enemy if attacked.

Terrible tails
Euoplocephalus (yoo-op-loh-sef-ah-lus) probably swung its hefty tail club from side to side.

A Euoplocephales tail club was a dangerous weapon!

Whippy weapon
Barosaurus (bar-oh-sore-us) may have used its long tail to lash out at its enemies.

Barosaurus could inflict a stinging blow with its tail.

Thin, bony plates stuck up from Stegosaurus's neck, back, and tail.

Plated protection
Stegosaurus (steg-oh-sore-us) was a huge dinosaur about the length of a truck! To put off predators, it had very tough skin and pointed, bony plates.

Kentrosaurus

Kentrosaurus was a member of the stegosaur family and lived in what is now eastern Africa. Its name means "sharp-point lizard". Its shoulders, back, and tail bore fearsome spikes that must have made it difficult for carnivores to attack it. Seven pairs of plates ran along *Kentrosaurus*'s neck and back. It had a pair of long spikes on its shoulders and a series of spikes along its tail to fend off attacks from behind.

Kentrosaurus's small head enclosed a tiny brain.

The snout and jaws were narrow, with a hornlike, toothless beak. It had small cheek teeth for grinding up plant food.

A flexible neck gave its head plenty of mobility for feeding.

This dinosaur is in a defensive crouch, but would normally have stood up straight.

44 **Why not find out more?**

The plates of bone on the back may have been used for display.

Predators trying to leap on Kentrosaurus or that were lashed by its tail risked being stabbed by its tail spikes and suffering fatal injuries.

The tail was very flexible (bendy). Kentrosaurus could swing it around to strike attackers on either side.

More than 900 *Kentrosaurus* bones were found in a single site in Tanzania.

www.dkfindout.com

Dinosaur facts

● Living relatives of dinosaurs, such as birds and crocodiles, show how some dinosaurs may have been coloured.

● The modern-day elephant is dull-coloured in much the same way as large, plant-eating dinosaurs may have been.

Markings break up an animal's outline so that they blend into the background.

Fading into forests

Large plant-eaters such as *Iguanodon* (ig-whan-oh-don) probably had green, scaly skin. Prowling predators would have found them hard to spot among the forest ferns!

Camouflage

The colouring of dinosaurs is unknown, but there are clues from today's animals. Dinosaurs were probably coloured and patterned for camouflage in their habitat.

Did Velociraptor pale skin with dark patches, like leopards?

… or black stripes on ginger, like tigers?

… or did it have feathers?

Lying in wait
Some meat-eating dinosaurs may also have had green or brown scaly skin. By blending into the background, they could sneak up on prey. See how this hunting crocodile looks like a log!

Predator in disguise
Velociraptor (vell-oss-ee-rap-tor) had long feathers, and looked like an eagle. Its colour would have matched its desert habitat.

Scaly story
Some dinosaurs had scales, while others had feathers. Dinosaur scales did not overlap. They fitted together like floor tiles.

Scales may have been different colours to form a pattern.

Bead-like scales vary in size and shape.

Looking leafy
Today's lizards also have scaly skins. Like *Iguanodon*, this iguana lives in leafy surroundings. Its emerald-green scales hide it from predators in its rainforest home.

Courtship

In the animal world, the strongest or most splendid-looking male has the best chance of attracting a female. Some dinosaurs may have challenged one another to trials of strength. Others showed off crests or frills.

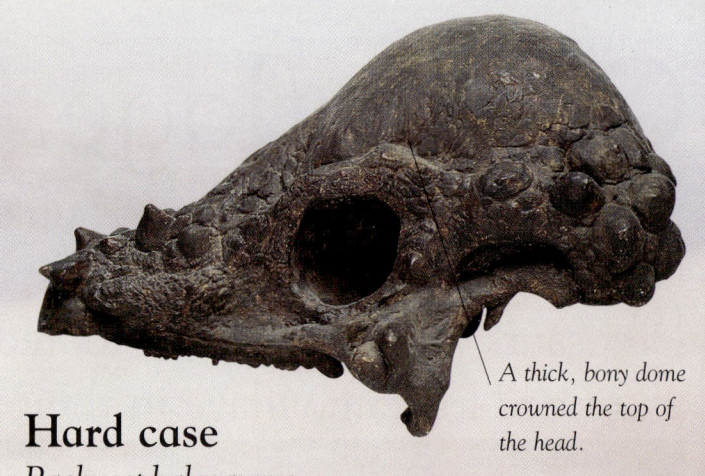

Hard case
Pachycephalosaurus (pack-ee-seff-allo-sore-us), the "thick-headed lizard", had a dome of thick bone on top of its head. Rival males may have head-butted or nodded to threaten each other.

A thick, bony dome crowned the top of the head.

Rival males may have shoved each other to show off their strength.

Battle of the boneheads
In dinosaur herds, males faced a lot of competition to win a mate. The strongest males were most likely to be chosen to father young. *Pachycephalosaurus* males perhaps battled it out head to head.

Dinosaur facts

- By choosing the winning males as mates, females chose healthy fathers for their young.
- *Pentaceratops* frills had skin-covered "windows" in the bone, creating spots of colour.
- *Corythosaurus* crests may have had amazing patterns.

Fantastic frills

Male *Pentaceratops* (pen-ta-serra-tops) had larger frills than the females. These were decorative, and males probably showed them off to attract a mate, or to frighten rival males.

Spiky skull

The vast neck frill of the "spiked lizard" *Styracosaurus* (sty rack-oh-sore us) was fringed with six spikes. Males may have used these to impress females.

Nose horn may have been used for jousting with rival males.

Colourful crests

Corythosaurus (ko-rith-oh-sore-us) had tall head crests. These were hollow, and helped produce trumpeting calls. Males' tall crests may also have scared off rival males, and impressed the females.

Locking horns

Like some dinosaurs, certain male mammals today seek to impress potential mates with displays of strength. Rams lock horns and try to push each other backwards. The one losing ground finally slinks away from the winner.

Nests and nurseries

Like most reptiles, dinosaurs laid eggs. Baby dinosaurs developed inside the egg. Some dinosaurs were caring parents. Others laid their eggs, then left their babies to fend for themselves.

Eggs and nests
Lots of dinosaurs laid their eggs in nests. Some nests were simple pits dug into the earth, whilst others were built with mud. The egg shells were brittle like those of birds' eggs, so that baby dinosaurs could break through them to hatch.

Parental protection
This *Citipati* (si-ty-pa-ty) died wrapped around her nest. She may have been trying to protect her brood. It is likely that she was smothered by wet sand. This probably happened during a rainstorm more than 80 million years ago.

Young Leallynasaura may have squawked to get their parents' attention!

Dinosaur facts

- *Maiasaura* (my-a-sore-a) means "good mother lizard". These gentle dinosaurs carefully looked after their babies when they were born.

- Some dinosaur eggs were tiny, yet the babies often grew into enormous creatures!

Happy families

Leaellynasaura (lee-el-in-a-sore-a) may have nested together in big groups like some seabirds do today. There is safety in numbers! After the eggs hatched, the parents probably looked after their babies for several months. It is likely they kept them warm and protected them from predators.

Parents probably brought food for the baby dinosaurs

High flyers

While dinosaurs roamed the land, the skies were ruled by flying reptiles called pterosaurs (ter-oh-sores). Large pterosaurs most likely flew over water, swooping down to catch fish. Smaller ones probably snapped up insects in the air.

Giant of the sky
The biggest flying animal that ever lived, *Quetzalcoatlus* (kwet-zal-koh-at-lus) was much heavier than a large human being. To support its weight, this Late Cretaceous pterosaur had a wingspan like that of a light aircraft.

Soaring over the sea
Pteranodon (ter-an-oh-don) used to glide over the Late Cretaceous seas. Its wings were ideal for soaring and also helped in swooping down for fish.

Bat wings
Like modern-day bats, pterosaurs had wings of leathery skin that stretched between their legs and fingers. Their bodies were covered in thick fur.

Sky diving
A Jurassic pterosaur, *Dimorphodon* (die-morf-oh-don) flapped its wings to fly. It hunted insects and small reptiles in woodlands.

Warm in all weather
To keep warm, the Late Jurassic *Sordes* (sor-deez) had a thick, hairy coat. It also had a long tail, almost as long as head, neck, and body combined.

Dinosaur facts

- The first-known bird was *Archaeopteryx* (ar-kee-op-terricks). It had feathers, wings, and a wishbone like a bird, but a reptile's teeth and bony tail.

- The modern-day hoatzin bird has claws on its wings. It uses these for climbing, like *Archaeopteryx* probably did.

- *Velociraptor* (vell-oss-ee-rap-tor) may have folded its arms sideways like wings. It had long feathers on its arms.

Eudimorphodon

Apart from dinosaurs, the most intriguing animals of the Mesozoic Era were the flying reptiles, or pterosaurs. Gliding on its leathery wings, *Eudimorphodon* was one of the first pterosaurs to take to the skies. It had a long tail and a short neck, and a pair of wings. It glided through the skies, snatching fish near the surface of the water and probably insects, too.

Its fourth fingers had stretched out, and together they formed the front edges of a pair of wings.

The long, bony tail may have had a diamond-shaped flap at the end to help it steer through the air.

54   **Why not find out more?**

Eudimorphodon had needlelike teeth at the tips of its jaws, plus many smaller teeth that formed long blades for slicing up prey.

The fingers of its hands had sharp claws.

Although similar to bat wings, Eudimorphodon's wings were more complex and possibly more efficient.

Eudimorphodon's terrifying long jaws had 110 teeth.

www.dkfindout.com 55

Under the waves

The world was much warmer when the dinosaurs lived, and there were no icebergs in the seas. Prehistoric oceans brimmed with a variety of other weird and wonderful reptiles.

Dinosaur facts
- Prehistoric seas teemed with familiar animals – fish, crabs, jellyfish, and snails.
- The prehistoric monsters of the deep were reptiles that came to the surface to breathe.
- Sea turtles and crocodiles survived the death of dinosaurs and sea reptiles.

Speedy swimmer
Ichthyosaurus (ick-thee-oh-sore-us), means "fish lizard". These reptiles looked like dolphins but swam like sharks, flicking their strong tails from side to side. They gave birth to live young under water.

Fearsome hunter
Liopleurodon (lie-oh-ploor-oh-don) had vast, powerful jaws that snapped shut on its unfortunate victims.

The enormous neck of Elasmosaurus grew up to 7 m (23 ft) long.

Shark survivors
Sharks have existed for millions of years. They have swum in the world's oceans before, during, and after the time of the dinosaurs.

Giant sea serpent

Elasmosaurus (ee-laz-moe-sore-us) had two pairs of flippers. It flapped these like wings to glide through the water. Females probably came ashore to lay their eggs in the sand, risking dinosaur attacks.

"Nessie", the Loch Ness monster

People claim to have seen a sea serpent swimming in Loch Ness in Scotland. "Nessie" is described as looking like an *Elasmosaurus*. Whatever killed the dinosaurs killed *Elasmosaurus*, too. But myth has it that Nessie still survives and hides in the depths of the Loch Ness!

Albertonectes

Albertonectes belonged to a group of marine reptiles known as plesiosaurs. It had a small head and a very long neck, and moved through the water by flapping its four long flippers. *Albertonectes*'s neck was much longer than the rest of its body. Scientists are not sure why this reptile needed such an incredibly long neck. It may have helped *Albertonectes* to pick animals such as shellfish off the seabed as it slowly swam forwards. *Albertonectes* probably also captured fish, squid, and other prey.

The eyes were adapted for good vision under water.

Albertonectes *might have had sharp, curved, conical teeth with long roots for strength.*

Why not find out more?

Albertonectes had a record-breaking 76 bones in its neck.

Each front flipper was a limb with the bones of five "fingers" supporting the broad paddle blade.

This animal has the longest neck of any plesiosaur discovered.

The back flippers had the same basic form as the front flippers.

The tail of this reptile was much shorter than its neck. It may have been equipped with a fin, which helped the animal turn while swimming.

www.dkfindout.com 59

Brain power

One way of measuring intelligence is to compare the size of the brain to the size of the body. It's likely that the dinosaurs that had bigger brains in relation to their body size were more intelligent than the others.

Small head housed a small brain.

Modern mammals like the tiger are near the top of the class for animal intelligence.

Not the smartest
Sauropods were less intelligent than most of the dinosaurs. Their heads were tiny compared to their vast bodies, with room for a small brain.

Birds are next in intelligence to mammals.

Less clever?
Some scientists believe that dinosaurs did not have the brain power of today's mammals and birds. However, they had enough brain power to survive successfully for millions of years.

Dinosaurs were perhaps less intelligent than today's birds.

Modern reptiles are less intelligent than some of the small hunting dinosaurs were.

The cleverest of all

A small hunter, *Troodon* (troh-o-don) had a large brain in relation to their body size. In fact, its brain was bigger than that of most other dinosaurs.

Dinosaur facts

- The size of a tall human being, *Troodon* had very large eyes. These helped it to hunt at dusk, and spot small prey.

- *Troodon* means "wounding tooth". It probably ate anything it could slash with its claws and tear apart with its teeth.

Dinosaur details

Citipati's huge oval eggs were bigger than a human hand!

Coelophysis is one of the earliest known dinosaurs to have a wishbone, just like a chicken!

The gigantic *Giraffatitan* weighed as much as six elephants!

The bite of a *Velociraptor* was as powerful as a lion's!

Why not find out more?

The average weight of *Iguanodon* was 3 tonnes, almost as much as two small cars!

Stegosaurus had one of the smallest brains of any dinosaurs relative to its body size. Its brain was half the size of a sheep's brain!

The skull of *Triceratops* is one of the biggest known among fossilized dinosaur skulls!

www.dkfindout.com

Death of the dinosaurs

Hundreds of different dinosaurs roamed the Earth 75 million years ago. Yet, 10 million years later, all (except the group that evolved into birds) died out. What happened is still uncertain.

Huge hollow
An enormous crater hidden in the Gulf of Mexico was caused by a giant asteroid hitting the Earth. The impact occurred 65 million years ago (around the same time that dinosaurs disappeared). It changed the Earth's atmosphere dramatically, and may well have led to the death of nearly all dinosaurs.

The asteroid would have hit the Earth at an incredible speed!

Deadly impact

The asteroid created a vast crater, similar to this one, when it hit the Earth. Huge clouds of rock and dust covered the Sun. These blocked out light and destroyed almost all plant life.

Dinosaur facts

- Birds of prey use their talons to seize food, just like some dinosaurs may have.

- An asteroid hitting the Earth may not have caused the dinosaurs to die out instantly. This probably occurred as the climate began to change.

When this dinosaur died, it was quickly buried under layers of mud and river sludge.

Survival of the toughest

Some animals lived through the changes in the Earth's atmosphere. Scorpions, turtles, birds, and insects were just some of the ones strong enough to survive!

In time, the layers covering the dinosaur turn to rock. The bones become incredibly hard over millions of years.

The wind and rain wear away the rock. Scientists discover the dinosaur bones and begin removing them from their tomb.

Rare reward

Fossils are the remains of things that lived long ago. Dinosaur fossils are a rare find. They are usually found in rock layers that formed at the bottom of swamps, lakes, or rivers.

Over a long period of time, movements deep within the Earth, force the skeleton towardsthe surface.

Buried bones

Removing dinosaur bones from a tomb of rock is a skilled job. Experts chip away carefully at the rock face to reveal bones that have not seen the light of day for millions of years.

Dinosaur facts

● The experts that dig up and rebuild dinosaur skeletons are called palaeontologists.

● Plant experts look for leaf remains in rock to learn about the prehistoric landscape.

● Fossilized droppings show what dinosaurs ate.

Digging up dinosaurs

Fossilized dinosaur bones can lie hidden in ancient rock. Dinosaur detectives, called palaeontologists (pay-lee-on-tol-oh-jist), search for buried fossils. Sometimes they find fossilized bones, teeth, and footprints. The most exciting finds are whole dinosaur skeletons.

Plaster protection
Palaeontologists wrap the dinosaur bones in bandages and runny plaster. This sets hard, protecting the surface of the bone like plaster casts protect broken legs.

Careful cleaning
The bones are taken to a museum where the plaster is cut away. They may even arrive still inside the rock. Cleaning the bones is a skilled job.

Prehistoric puzzle
Rebuilding a prehistoric skeleton from a jumble of bones is a tricky task. It is like putting together a difficult jigsaw puzzle!

Palaeontologists piece together a Pliosaurus *skeleton.*

Building dinosaurs

Rebuilding a dinosaur is a lengthy process. Fossilized bones are removed from ancient rock. Experts then make a copy of these. Getting the replica bones ready for display is quite complicated and can take a long time!

Making the mould
An expert begins by carefully painting each of the fossilized bones with liquid rubber. When the rubber dries, it makes a flexible mould.

Putting it all together
The moulds are removed from the bones and coated in liquid plastic. This forms the outside of the replica skeleton.

Each limb bone is moulded in two halves.

Filling the bones!
Liquid plastic is poured inside the hollow moulds. This sets into a stiff foam.

Finishing touches
The outer moulds are removed to reveal the replica bones. They are pieced together and painted to look like real bones. The replica skeleton is then displayed for everyone to see!

Recreating the past

This lifesize copy of a *Barosaurus* (barrow-sore-us) skeleton is displayed in a New York museum. Metal rods are welded together to keep it in position. It is mounted on a supporting metal frame.

Guide ropes keep the replica steady as it is moved into position.

This replica is over 15 m (49 ft) high. It towers over visitors to the museum!

This Barosaurus is shown rearing up on its hind legs!

Index

armour 42
asteroids 64-65

baby dinosaurs 50-51
bats 53, 55
beaks 6-7, 13, 21, 22, 30, 36, 37, 44
bird-hipped dinosaurs 12-13
birds 2, 7, 12-13, 46, 53, 60, 64, 65
bones 9, 12, 28, 31, 45, 48, 49, 59, 65, 66-67, 68,
brains 6, 7, 13, 44, 60-61

camouflage 46-47
claws 2, 3, 28, 30, 42, 53, 55, 61
colours 46-47, 49
continents 4-5
courtships 48-49
crests 25, 48, 49
Cretaceous period 4, 5, 7, 12, 13, 15, 24, 26, 31, 52
crocodiles 2, 46, 47, 56
cycads 15, 21

death of dinosaurs 56, 64-65
defence 6, 25, 42
dragonflies 15
duck-billed dinosaurs 14, 24

eggs 11, 30, 50-51, 57, 62
eyes 9, 22, 24, 58, 61

ferns 14-15, 20, 46
flowering plants 14-15
flying reptiles 3, 52-53, 54
footprints 10-11, 19, 67
fossils 6, 7, 8-9, 11, 15, 32, 63, 65, 66-67, 68
frills 48-49

Gondwana 4

herds 24-25, 48
hip bones 12
horns 3, 6, 7, 13, 25, 28, 49

insects 15, 65
intelligence 60-61

jaws 2, 6, 9, 14, 21, 27, 28, 30, 44, 55, 56
Jurassic period 4-5, 13, 21, 28, 53, 67

Laurasia 4
legs 2, 3, 4, 6, 7, 16, 18, 19, 20, 29, 31

lizard-hipped
  dinosaurs 12-13
lizards 2, 12, 13, 30, 47
Loch Ness monster 57

mammals
  15, 30, 49, 60
meat-eating dinosaurs 2,
  3, 4, 19, 26-27, 30-31, 47
  claws 3, 28, 30, 61
  colours 47
  hunting 3, 30-31
  teeth 2, 3, 27, 28,
  58, 61

Mesozoic 4, 54
monkey-puzzle trees
  15
movement 18-19
nests 11, 50-51
noises 24-25

oceans 56

palaeontologists 66-67
Pangaea 4
Panthalassa 4
plant-eating dinosaurs 12,
  15, 20-21, 25, 42, 46
  colours 47
  herds 24-25
  size 3, 21
  teeth 14, 21, 23, 44
plants 14-15

predators 26, 28, 31,
  42, 43, 47
reptiles 2, 3, 5, 9, 50,
  52-53, 54, 56, 58

scales 47
sea reptiles 56-57, 58-59
sharks 56
skeletons 6-7, 66-67,
  68-69
skin 2, 3, 8, 43, 46-47
stomachs 21

tails 2, 3, 6, 7, 19, 20,
  23, 29, 42, 43, 44-45,
  53, 54, 56, 59
teeth 2-3, 6, 14, 21,
  23, 27, 28, 41, 42, 44,
  53, 55, 58, 61
Triassic period 4

weapons 42-43
whales 3
wings 52-53, 54-55
wolf 31

71

Acknowledgements

Dorling Kindersley would like to thank:
Hilary Bird for preparing the index; Jon Hughes for digital illustrations; Andrew O'Brien for additional digital artwork p.20; Clare Shedden and Mo Choy for design assistance; Rachel Hilford for picture library services; and Fleur Star for editorial assistance with the activity pages.

Picture credits

The publisher would like to thank the following for their kind permission to reproduce their photographs:
(Key: a-above; b-below/bottom; c-centre; f-far; l-left; r-right; t-top)

American Museum Of Natural History: D Finnin 50tr; J Beckett 30tl; **Bruce Coleman Ltd:** Bruce Coleman Inc 18-19; Dr Hermann Brehm 12-13; Gordon Langsbury 2tl, 3tl; Jeff Foott 49br; Jens Rydell 26; Jules Cowan 4tl; Pacific Stock 56bc; Tore Hagman 20. **getty images stone:** 16-17; Darryl Torckler 57. **Corbis:** Tom Bean 10-11; **Dorling Kindersley:** The American Museum of Natural History 36-37bc, 37cb, 49cl; Senckenberg Gesellshaft Fuer Naturforschugn Museum 33bc; Centaur Studios - modelmaker 37bl; Graham High at Centaur Studios - modelmaker 36cr, 36crb, 39tl; Jon Hughes 35cr, 38cra, 38cl, 38cb, 38bl, 38bc, 39tr, 39ca, 39cr, 39crb, 39bl; **Natural History Museum, London,** 9t, 39br; Peter Minister, Digital Sculptor 35tl, 36bc, 37tc; Royal Tyrrell Museum of Palaeontology, Alberta, Canada 36cra; Senckenberg Gesellshaft Fuer Naturforschugn Museum 37ca, 37ca (*Stegosaurus*); State Museum of Nature, Stuttgart 37c; Natural History Museum: 19tl, 48tr, 49tr. **Dreamstime.com:** Nickolay Stanev 18-19 (Background) **N.H.P.A.:** Daniel Heuclin 14, 30-31; John Shaw 46-47; Kevin Schafer 14br, 42; Martin Wendler 2bl, 3bl, 61; **Oxford Scientific Films:** 25tr; Daniel J Cox 31tr; Mark Deeble and Victoria Stone 2bl; **Planet Earth Pictures:** M & C Denis Huot 25cla; Royal Tyrell Museum Canada: 7tc, 7br, 12cb, 12c, 21br, 61crb; **Science Photo Library:** Francois Gohier 65tl; Jim Amos 66; Julian Baum 64tr; Peter Menzel 67c; Philippe Plailly 67tr, 67cla; Photo library International/ESA/SPL 64bl; Senekenberg Nature Museum: 6ca, 6c, 6-7cb; State Museum of Nature 6tr; **Woodfall Wild Images:** A Leemann 4bc; Alan Watson 24; Heinrich van den Berg 19tr; Ted Mead 47cla.

All other images © Dorling Kindersley
For further information see:
www.dkimages.com